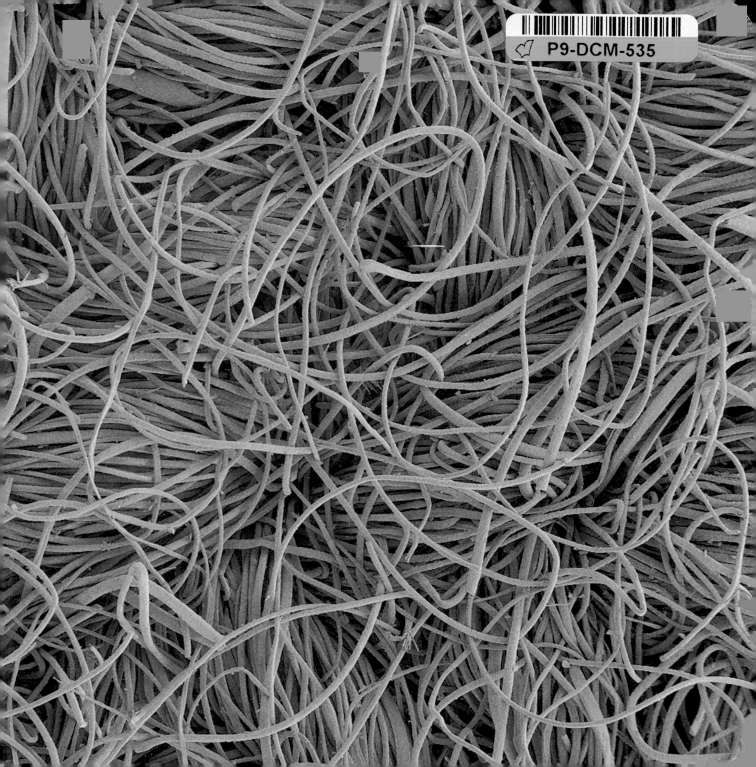

Text copyright © 2017 by Idan Ben-Barak
Illustrations copyright © 2017 by Julian Frost
Scanning electron microscope images by Linnea Rundgren
A Neal Porter Book
Published by Roaring Brook Press
Roaring Brook Press is a division of Holtzbrinck Publishing Holdings
Limited Partnership
175 Fifth Avenue, New York, NY 10010
mackids.com

Library of Congress Control Number: 2017957291
ISBN: 978-1-250-17536-6

Our books may be purchased in bulk for promotional, educational, or
business use. Please contact your local bookseller or the Macmillan Corporate
and Premium Sales Department at (800) 221-7945 ext. 5442 or by e-mail
at MacmillanSpecialMarkets@macmillan.com.

First published in Australia in 2017 by Allen & Unwin
First American edition, 2018

Printed in China by RR Donnelley Asia Printing Solutions Ltd.,
Dongguan City, Guangdong Province

3   5   7   9   10   8   6   4   2

Do not lick this book*

IDAN BEN-BARAK and JULIAN FROST

SCANNING ELECTRON MICROSCOPE IMAGES
by LINNEA RUNDGREN

A Neal Porter Book

Roaring Brook Press / New York

* IT'S FULL
OF GERMS.

This is Min.

Min is a microbe. She's small. Very small.
Can you see this dot?

•

Microbes are so small that 3,422,167[*]
of them could fit on it.

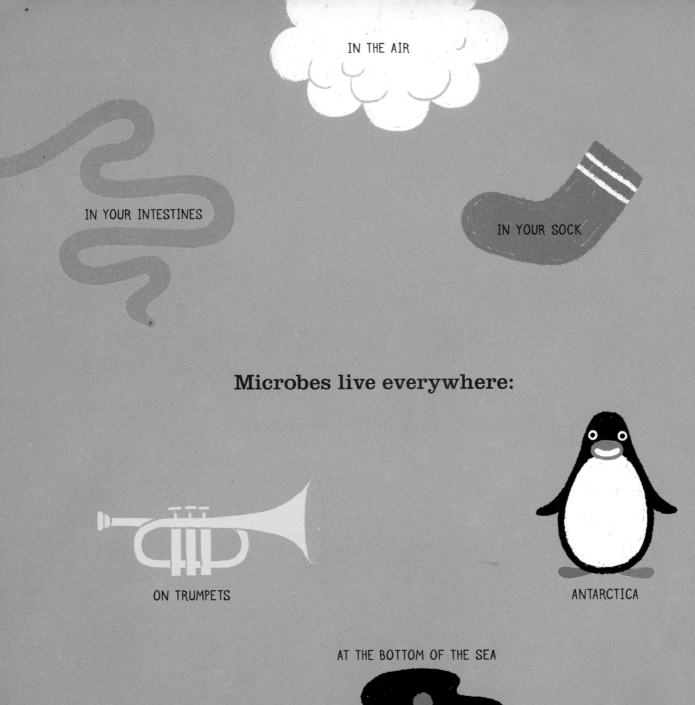

IN THE AIR

IN YOUR INTESTINES

IN YOUR SOCK

Microbes live everywhere:

ON TRUMPETS

ANTARCTICA

AT THE BOTTOM OF THE SEA

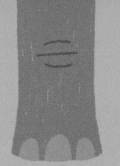

ON ELEPHANTS' KNEES

JUST OVER THERE

UNDERGROUND

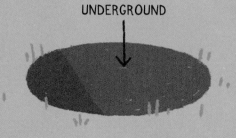

IN YOUR BREAKFAST

INSIDE THIS FISH

UP SANTA'S NOSE

ON TOP OF MOUNT EVEREST

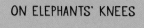

Let's take Min on an adventure!
See the circle on the next page?
That's where Min lives. Touch the circle
with your finger to pick her up.

Min lives in this book.
And if you could look

really

really

closely...

. . . you'd see her.

I'M BORED.

This is a photo of paper, really, really close up.

Let's take Min on an adventure!

See the circle on the next page?
That's where Min lives. Touch the circle
with your finger to pick her up.

Min is now on your finger!

Where shall we take Min first?

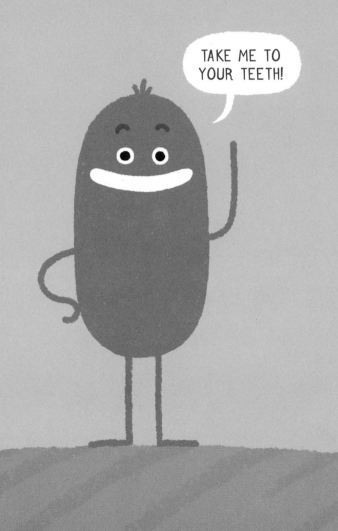

Okay, let's go.

Open your mouth and carefully touch
your front teeth with your finger.

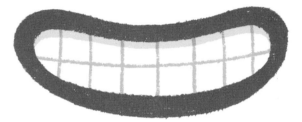

Now let's look

really,

really

closely...

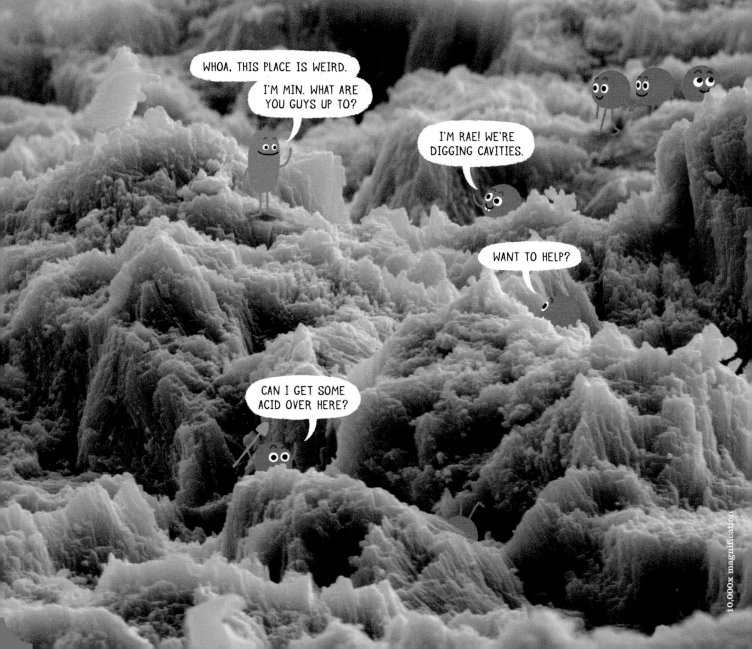

This is a photo of a tooth, really, really close up.

10,000x magnification

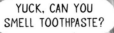

What a strange place teeth are
when you look really, really closely.
No wonder it's a good idea to brush them.

It's time for Min's next adventure.
Touch your teeth to pick Min up.

Looks like you've picked up Rae as well.
Where shall we go next?

All right, let's explore your shirt.

Put your finger on your shirt to send
Min and Rae on a new adventure.

Now let's look

really,

really

closely...

This is a photo of fabric, really, really close up.
I'M MIN AND THIS IS RAE. WE'RE ON AN ADVENTURE.
ADVENTURE!
NICE TO MEET YOU. MY NAME'S DENNIS.
WE'RE MAKING THIS SHIRT SMELL.
GROSS. I FOUND A CLEAN PATCH.
DENNIS, THERE'S SOME LOVELY FILTH DOWN HERE!
350x magnification

What a strange place shirts are
when you look really, really closely.
No wonder they need washing.

Now it's time for Min and Rae's next adventure.
Touch your shirt to pick them up.

Dennis has come along for the ride.
We have time for one more trip.
Where shall we go?

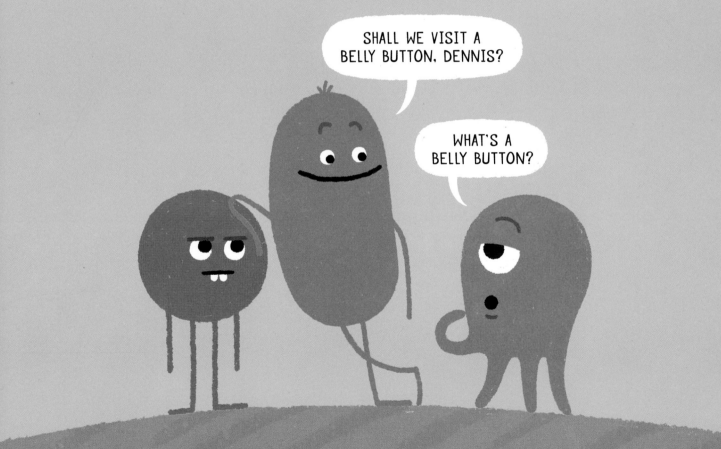

Okay, off we go!

Put your finger in your belly button
and wiggle it about.

Now let's look

really,

really

closely . . .

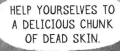

What a strange place skin is
when you look really, really closely.
No wonder it gets itchy.

Put your finger back in your belly button
to pick up Min and her friends.

Let's put Min and her friends
back in this book.

Here's a good spot!

There's plenty of room for everyone.

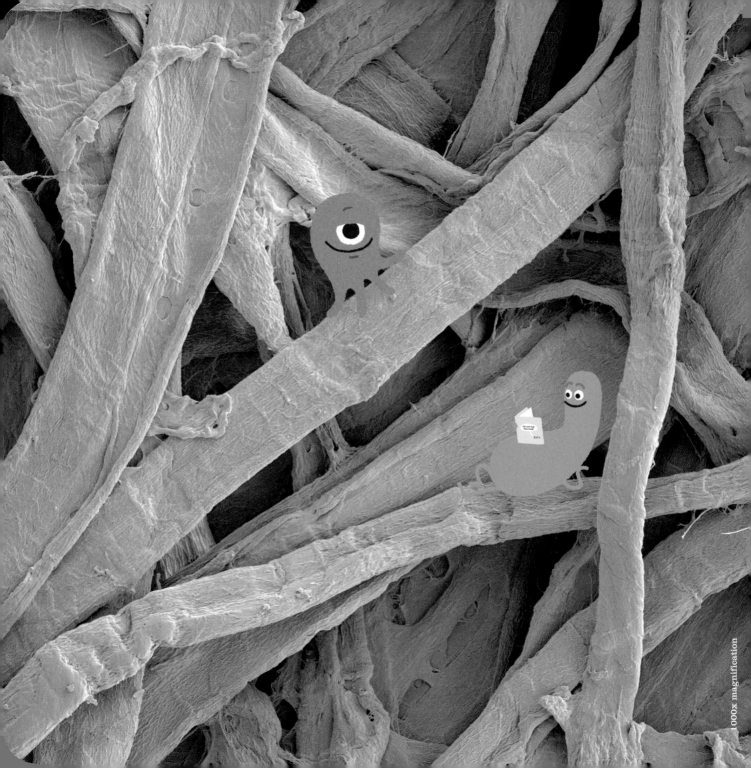

Where will you take Min tomorrow?

What microbes really look like

Microbes are so small that nobody knew they even existed until microscopes were invented. They come in all sorts of odd shapes, but they don't have faces, feet, or hands, and they can't really talk. Sorry, Min.

Min is an E. coli

E. coli live happily in your intestines, but they are very good at spreading, especially when you don't wash your hands too well.

Rae is a streptococcus

Streptococcus bacteria live in lots of places, including your mouth, eating sugar and pooping acid that can dissolve your teeth.

Dennis is a fungus

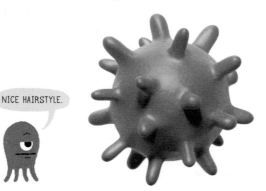

His real name is *Aspergillus niger*. You probably picked him up while playing outside.

Jake is a corynebacterium

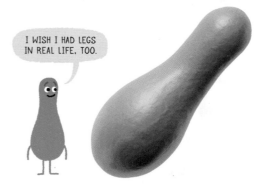

Corynebacteria live on lots of places, including your skin. They're big fans of dirt.

What the people who made this book look like

IDAN BEN-BARAK

Idan wrote most of the words.
He's usually found inside
libraries. He sometimes thinks
quite loud thoughts.

JULIAN FROST

Julian drew the pictures.
He likes comics and toast.
He once animated a video called
"Dumb Ways to Die."

LINNEA RUNDGREN

Linnea took the microscope photos.
She uses complicated machines to
look at very, very tiny things and
extremely big things. There are
patterns everywhere.